Songs from the Multiverse

poems by

M. L. Lyons

Finishing Line Press
Georgetown, Kentucky

Songs from the Multiverse

ACKNOWLEDGMENTS

Grateful acknowledgment also to the following journals and editors who created a
space for these poems:

Alluvian: "Nocturne"
Assisi: An Online Journal of Arts and Letters: "The Passion of St. Francis"
Beaverton Arts Commission Website for World Poetry Day: "If Peace Was a Postcard"
Between the Lines: "The Dragon Sutra" and "Unfathered"
Cedar Mills Anthology 2023: "Leaf Horn"
Crab Creek Review: "Hercules Capturing the Ceryneian Hind"
The Ekphrastic Review: "On De Kooning's 'Woman and Bicycle'"
InSpiritry: Art of Peace Poetry Anthology: "Peace is a refugee..."
Phrasings Festival 2014 Chapbook for Chuckanut Sandstone Writers and Bellingham
Dance Repertory Company: "Red Temple Heart"
Poetry of the Wild Flowers: "Heart of the Earth"
Raven Chronicles: "Miles Davis's 'Sketches of Spain'"
Terrain.org: "The Wall That Walked Away"
Tiny Seed Literary Journal: "Nymphalidae"
Written River: A Journal of Eco-Poetics: "Cairn" and "Song of the Ice Snake"

Publisher: Leah Huete de Maines
Editor: Christen Kincaid
Cover Art: Greg Camenzind
Author Photo: Greg Camenzind
Cover Design: Elizabeth Maines McCleavy

Order online: www.finishinglinepress.com
also available on amazon.com

Author inquiries and mail orders:
Finishing Line Press
PO Box 1626
Georgetown, Kentucky 40324
USA

Contents

Not only is the Universe stranger than we think,
it is stranger than we can think.

—Werner Heisenberg

The Wall That Walked Away

(Inspired by Andy Goldsworthy's piece, "The Wall That Went for A Walk" and Norman Nicholson's "Wall")

I will not fortify or fence your neighbor's plot.
For under us all ground does give
and though I press each roughshod hoof,
I quiver, as round the ribbings of my rocks,
each root probes through sod and soil.
Vines creep and crown my back,
and twist flowers into my craggy mane.

You make your walls to stand erect and stay.
Each soldier brick upright or layered hard to hold.
Your mausoleums and your mansions fast in place.
I'll canter and strut my knob-kneed way
past bewildered farmers in their fields.
I'm wandering this watching world.
Past parcels, past roads, past what you claim is space.

I'll make each church surrender to the sky.
Create transparent spires for your faith.
Undam your rivers. Unbuckle every boulder
of your battlements and release the rubble
plundered, that groaning weight of gold and gains.
Run past rivulets, breaking flank by flank,
until what's wild rises up to me, and you will see
each bud and bird and beast burst forth into its proper dignity.

Cairn

Place is found by walking.
—Andy Goldsworthy

My touch is
timed to wind and
wave. Each brick seasoned
by the sun. This pyre of earth,
rock, and wood will not last an
age. Conifer of umber. Teardrop
of stone. Rain-hammered, wind-
worn, spanned by a man's reach.
This sandstone egg glows red,
dwarfing the plain. It grows.
Its falling shows Nature
is not small. I grip this
earth only so long.

Song of the Ice Snake

Snakes are the perfect sculptural form... they draw the path they are taking.
    —*Andy Goldsworthy*

I am the path I am taking. Meaning ripples into
place. Cool as your ancestral caves, the first arches
you ever entered. Look how I curl across this naked branch.
I can echo every shape. Even the muscling earth slips between
my vertebrae. I bend and slide, rise above your riverbed
to treetops, then drape the earth's stones in a sinuous embrace.
I am the stilled waters you always wanted to taste.
I smooth all paths and settle all the angled arguments of your race.

Rain Shadow

We are elemental—you and I.
Our shadows lengthen or shorten according
to the light a graying sky casts.
Laying down on these stones,
I wait for the wind to change its voice.

Rain is unbounded.
It opens everything.
The world I believed I held
slips between my fingers
into an earth rich and rivering.

After the storm, I will rise
and see what is left of me.
A white chalk-like form. A shadow reversed.
Stepping away, I take a picture.
A shadow keeping shadows after the rain.

Leaf Horn

Standing here, bent over

  sweet chestnut leaves enfolded

    on the grass, curved then pinned by thorns,

      shaped like the tender horns of a young ram,

       borne out of a wet-green spring,

        an emerald nautilus composed of earthly things.

        Holding within itself that subtle rustle,

       the memory of what leaves

       the sweep and curl of its fall

      with its amberish yellows and

       ginger reds rusting into

           umber and deeper still,

       the agate green whisper of

      each tree branching into spring.

      This is the great spiral of sound that

     stems from this world. Far flung and formless,

    the heartbeats of a thousand things. Witness its wave

   and crackle. Its listless billow and drift.

  All these wavering moments.

 Delicate and immortal as swallow wings.

No need to sound the horn.

It already sings.

Nymphalidae

In other tongues, we flicker closer to your flight—
parvaneh, papillon, mariposa—
the soft undulance of words plush with quiver
and unrestrained delight.
Part bird, part flower, full wing.

See your black bent body
warming in the sun.
Every leg winding down
over the wetness of pink petals to pistils.
A soft smudge of tawny pollen
brushed against your backside.
How each palp can suck sweetness from mud.
All the salts and honeyed nectars curling
and captured in your tonguish mouth.

Sometimes you outwit what preys on you,
you draw back and form a fan
of false beige eyes or turn
to tendril green, and watch the predator
see owl, see leaf, sense nothing
of what you are underneath.

Imagine the pleasurable burst of your birth,
pearly drops flung freely, then pressed
against the ribbed undersides of leaves.
A trace of silvery beads laid long
after hours spent mating what felt like sky.

Behold the composition of colors encased
in that silken sac. Vermillion lines, sulphurous
moons, greenish deltas of lakes and yellows fashioned
from the sun. All in that dun chrysalis, breathless,
brown and still. Your puffed, articulated skin grows tight
to feed the stranger self within.

So, when you break along that fine ridge
called back, we cannot hear that stemmed body
snap and you alone, parvaneh, papillon,
mariposa, psyche's wings, know how
you wrought yourself to spring.

Nocturne

Blue blooded monarch, triple hearted, fluidly unspools
herself to wind, then unwinds
stretching across the sea with the throbs of time.

Liquid sac of sentience, her mind feels through the dark deep.
The sea, with its perpetual twilight indigoed
from eons of volcanic floods and the endless silt of nameless rivers.

She is a rainbow of tactility regenerating herself
at will, wearing the sea's dreams
like a shy queen, with her endless handkerchief drops.

Now, she glides through vast colonnades of graying membraned coral,
emptied and eerie with silence, seeking a darkened nest,
some sheltered crag to brood and birth her private treasure of tear dropped eggs.

Each tentacle as mindful as the next, she tastes the ocean's burgeoning brine
and feels an odd prickle of silvery pressure,
inescapable now, for she is carried only so far by the currents.

Clinging to the rock face, she curtains her eggs in long, opalescent strings,
refreshing each globe with air,
before covering her clutch of eggs under her mantle.

She braids each glossy drop within the blanching bracelet of her arms
until she whitens into trembling tatters
that lace the drift and flow and settle upon the ocean bed's remains.

Since she cannot, perhaps each lucent head, all innocent ebony eyes it seems, will rim
the waves and member and remember to entwine its genes
and find that sovereign, solitary gesture to save itself and so survive this age.

The Vanishing

The question is, are we happy to suppose that our grandchildren may never see an elephant except in a picture book?
— Richard Attenborough

She is leaving the aerial spiral of mobiles above our babies' beds, and
    fading from the memory of animal crackers in our children's hands.
Now, she has slipped out from their tight grasp. She is their bedside familiar, and yet
    she is climbing far away, out of our storybooks, as her image falls from the pages.
She is silenced in the wet vowels of our children's first alphabet and has
    lost her place among our long menageries of miniatures.

She has left the field of the great maps in our ivory towers and relinquished her foothold
    on the borders of every continent. Her tread will weigh no more upon the land.
She has walked from the bright fanfare of endless circus rings, slipping
    out of those colossal chains, and stepped down from the high mount of graying heads.

She has left the low cages of eternal display, lost to the world of point and look.
    Vanishing from the green, luminescent dioramas, she exits the familiar histories
    we have known. No longer imagined where she once stood in greatness
        among ancestors, ancient and primeval.
All traces of her chiseled figure are being erased from the temples we once made in her honor.
        She has gathered herself up, no longer ground into the fading powders of aphrodisiacs.
She is leaving the hammers of tinkling keys, ending the music we made of her.

A Shimmer of Hope

In the midst of the worst fires we'd ever seen,
they came and visited us, a godsend, a sign
that not all would be lost even as
the alder outside trembled in dismay
and its leaves twisted into grey claws,
struggling to breath out the mess we'd made.
Even the evergreen gave its needles up and cast
its cones in a hallowed circle, hoping for resurrection.

What, the world asks, could possibly survive us?

Still, they came, a shimmer
of hummingbirds. Each as determined as the next,
ruby-throated, green-throated, full of thirst.
Their nearly transparent wings relentlessly
whirring against the smoky breath,
and we fed them, as if in apology.

Frozen Radiance

Here is the antiquity of ice. The beauty of
seemingly infinite ice, its pristine layers of preservation in crisp limestone.
Blue, then bluer than blue moving through time's spectrum.
Paled turquoise, twenty, frosted malachite, a hundred,
sapphire blue, thousands, then to crystalline moon blue, a million years back,
preserving each moment—

How sweet the air where the first forests swelled into life.
How full, the volcanic plumes billowed across Pangaea's wonder.
And in the purest azure, locked in its translucent self—
the memories of magnificent meteorite showers, their flow lines edging
the sky, arcing their singular ways—iron yellow, violet and teal
until their inevitable magnetism drew them
down like fireworks' traces.

All these inexorable pressings of snow and ice,
compressed into some monolithic memory book, each
snowflake flattened to the size of a footprint. They hold tight the crystalline.
The keepsakes of this earth.

Here are the species of ice: frazil, grease, nilas to gray.
Hump backed, or horned, domed or sloped, peaked with pinnacles,
Surges and flows, retreating as we enter and then vanish into the ocean.

Listen to the glaciers, as they groan and calve,
Watch them as they break into white—the color of young ice—
emerging as their interior selves.

With a crack, all their hidden gothic cathedrals rise then collapse
into waters of seawater jade, black with sediment or mountain silt blue.
Capturing and refracting every light with their mirrored lengths of water.
Continents away, we watch, but do not listen.

This is the mind of winter.
How long the path of light saving time into itself.
Being time. Being ice and yet so scattered. Time being time. Self-time.
Cooling and absorbing. Cooling and holding. Cooling and steadying the warmth of things.

Icebergs shrinking to snow covers to snowmelt,
water flowing to the rivers and streams,
back again to the maternal ocean with its sea green possibilities.

Now, the melt flows in turbulent pulses, cascading in a gush of loss,
falling into the ocean's arms.

This is the soul of ice.
Ice speaking to the ocean, water to water. Sympathetic in their resonances.
Ice cools the jet streams of the oceans beneath.
Water, the shapeshifter of us all.

Heart of the Earth

I am the amethyst studded stalk of self-heal.
You have named me well—blue earth, heart-of-the-earth
healing the hurt of the world with my purple dressings.
Generosity fills every part of me.
Place these mint gray leaves upon your wounds
and they will heal and bear no scar.
Soak and steep each flowering point, each rising stalk
and hope will surge within you as your fevers subside.
I travel the world seed by seed. Strengthening your streambanks.
I adorn your neglected roadsides, clothe your fields
desolate in the blistering sun, your disturbed clearings full of debris,
I give them the green softness of life, our true inheritance.
I will walk in beauty there. Flowering humbly,
only wanting nearness to this earth, to this sweet ground.

O Bright Star!

What was it you first held so tenderly in your fists?
What lit your dreams then? Did you listen like a nascent moon?
Did you wonder at this world-womb?
Were all senses luminous in those long, unlit slumbers of darkness?
Were you circling around cloudlessness?
What quickening stirred you from your warm infant cradle?
What starry globe filled your eyes, clearer than the sky?
What nameless rose petaled within you when you finally woke?
Was it all more wonder-filled than you could dream?
And as you entered, when did you see the otherness of this place?

The Passion of St. Francis

When I cast off my brocade robe and my father's
          love with it, the color of scarlet flamed in his tightened
fist and I saw how naked was the world and even
          the arthritic bishop's hand quivered on my shoulder
with the words I said and I knew the season of lilies was
          at hand like the fingers of the leper whom I refused
to help when I watched him crouching a gray bundle raveling
          away his skin and I turned my horse towards him and
felt the ravages of fear I had within, and I knew that
          to pass this man was precious loss so I pressed my stallion
forward tiny bells on its girdle and I saw then the sweetness of the
          wedding banquet I would miss and the scent of jasmine and
roses my bride would never wear or the pleasures of
          the bed when at dawn I would admire her lengths of auburn hair
and I watched the stallion's nostrils flare at the stink of his flesh
          while the road twisted towards him and the stones
rang like the armor I once wore and the cups of wine I spilled into
          my lover's faithless lips soft and darting as the stars and how
I plotted for so little when my father's men cried out as I reckless
          sold the gentling folds of amber satin and velvet bolts
from my father's hoard to women hungry for the feel of small
          pleasures and stepping down I saw how his begging bowl
rimmed with sunlight shone beside his gnawed hand and how in
          his eyes rheumy with sickness there a church rubbled now
rose and hidden from my face I divined something simpler how
          stone by stone I might sing a sanctuary into place
crying out repair repair and bless the canticles of this face this sun
          and kiss embrace the body blessed and bowed
until such miracles in time when in the shadow's silence
          all things are drawn to my breast and the snowy paw of a wolf
hungry for flesh would one day rest within my outstretched palm.

Unfathered

St. Francis Bacon, painter
knew the fleshy crush of love,
its bootless screams.
Hidebound, tethered by hooks to
his sore embattled body,
he knew the bristling burn of making meat.
His father coarsened his shame,
fired the stablehand,
gave the boy a roasting slap
before unfathering him.
No son of mine does things like that.
And Bacon, barely sixteen, crawled
about the barn, suffered his violent
visions as fists and hooves
came crashing down.

Hercules Capturing the Ceryneian Hind

(After Michael C. Spafford's murals, "The Twelve Labors of Hercules")

Pursuing a hind into the falling sun and rising moon,
he felt its heat, the pride of golden
antlers tumbling over his privates, the stag's
head lolling, how its weight sunk into his shoulders,
feebly kicking like a young virgin, relinquishing itself,
the long race through the blackberry
bush and bramble, finally over, its brown eyes
locked in space, its lashes, womanly,
fine musky scent and sweat glistening on its body.

He would miss the shadows of
the forest, the shelter of conifers.
He who could outrun the very sun.
He'd long for the shadows turning into
traces themselves, the cool evening breeze,
running, not even seeing, the light
hoof prints, the way the grasses tremble
under its gentle stamping, the quick dart
and leap, a tender crescent arc under
the widening eye of the moon.

On De Kooning's "Woman and Bicycle"

Art never seems to make me peaceful or pure. I always seem
to be wrapped in the melodrama of vulgarity. I do not
think... of art as a situation of comfort.
        —Willem de Kooning

Between the brush and his brain he finds her.
The tittering click of heels and gossip.
Unstable as a bauble's swing.
Her soft perfumed sway unsettles
the senses.

Full of chartreuse sentiments,
bringing in the evening mail with full coverage.
Slyer than a nettle's sting, she knows the art
of a prying glance, the way a woman has
with news rife with innuendoes.

The slap of recognition, the smart
red conversational twist, engorged
with spite. She is sex self-dilated,
dominating an entire landscape,
legs askew for anyone's delight.

Her breasts the soft machinery
of motherhood gone to waste. Her mind,
a boxed heirloom awaiting use,
its meaning rattled into place.

Her eyes, the color of tumbled
quartz—milky, prone to tears.
Her mouth freshly shredded with
the hard gleam of ivories loosely strung.

She is a woman made
and then made undone.

Miles Davis's 'Sketches of Spain'

The melodic phrase begins to pry open the mystery of the tones and remove the precious stone of the sob,
a resonant tear on the river of the voice. That is 'duende.'
—*Federico Garcia Lorca*

Miles, you understood the delirium of beauty, how well it plays
with pain. Music transfixes a moment into memory
fusing tones with pieces of time.

Notes as drenched with *duende* as the eddies of the East River,
gunmetal grey, unveiling the slope of a shoulder, some suicide lost
in the city's sway. A sunset suffused with darkness.

It takes a strong wind to play a strong trumpet, you whispered, voice riven
by that same constricted breath. Bracing against that same wind, you played,
your back turned to them, saying *who do you think I play for?*

Miles, you lived for years alone in this city. Hermit brewing dark notes
pure as your wide-eyed glare. Anyone could go a little mad here.
Seven flights up and there's all the exile you ever wanted.

Your notes spirited through the air, past empty rooms, past all
   those session men in streets neon brilliant with indifference
      all night… for sale… name your price…

You knew how this city can claim everything,
   even what feels like your soul, when you nightwalked by
      Paradise Drugs, and in the window, saw your face multiply.

I burned too in the city, not from a needle, but from its relentless
   tricks, the nameless grasp of my ankle or when a phantom of a woman
      wove her fingers into my hair because she liked its feel.

Your notes washed away all those nameless hauntings, entered the soles
   of my feet, vein by vein, covering me with a veil of black notes until I emerged
      shimmering, as if I'd seen, unblinded, the gold corona of an eclipsed sun.

The Dragon Sutra

Ringed by a wintry rockbound shore,
            I watch the bewildering sand rise
       then seep beneath my feet.
    I feel the shuddering thunder welt
               the sky, and I cannot leave the heaving
          sea, but look into its vaporous foam,
     and in the wrestling waters see
         as my gaze grows, the ocean's jaws unleash
                       a legion of limbs and claws and teeth.
A dragon knows how scepters
           swivel into swords then sink
   into a flag's deafening defeat,
        how wildness misnamed, seizes
                both the tyrant and the lord,
        this wormy truth, this scaly thing.
    And I watch its fowlish wings,
         shadowing the shore,
          dripping, resplendent, golden
             claws, half-moon fingered king
      as walls of marbled waves stand still
      until it becomes my breath, and I grow serpentine
    and it breathes mine and
      I grow my ripening
             wings.

Red Temple Heart

Ink dries on her body
as his hand moves across her
like moonlight over water.

Her eyes dwell on his. In his.
One mind passes to another.
When he offers as a promise
of love, a silver bowl filled with snow,
his lips bloom into a red cup.
Thirsty, always thirsty.

An old man tenderly rests beside
three plum blossom trees.
Reclining there,
he hears the sky branching out
to hold the weight
of each white crane's cry.

Pouring warm water over his curved
back, steam rises and turning to her,
he is a child again, black lashes beaded
with water. Their bodies leaf,
bending towards the light.

Her breath unfolds in the mist, weaving
into the air like threads of incense.
Tears falling like the jade needles of
pines tracing their shadows
on a doorstep.

Zeami and the Demon Meet on a Wintry Night

Zeami (1363-1443), founder of Japanese Noh drama, was exiled to the island of Sado because of court intrigues. Two years before his death, the court allowed him to return to Kyoto.

The demon has the sure subtlety of stamping
    one foot. And the rattle of brown beads, cajoling,
is in the hands of a shaken traveler, hungry for home.
    One man forced to wander far by fate. One man wandering far by force.
For demon has spoken his wintry tale and the traveler is wending
    through the riven winter night. With each longing rush of
wind, the pines bend bright with snow.
    The demon cries, *Lost. Lost. No place to call my own.*
Zeami nods, *Exile is when you meet your greatest foe... alone.*
    Alone in the shadows of the wood, the demon's eyes glisten bright.
From out of the darkness have I come. See my robe is filled with light.
    The man's mind is whispering too, with the branches, with the snow.
For silence is the proper place where every mystery grows.

Speak

I am a stranger in this place.

They write in sand, and I gesture back in palms.
I say beauty and oasis. I offer rivulets of amber dripping from a honeycomb.

The men ask where do you come from?
I say mother tree raises us all, and she is generous.

The children laugh and ask what she tastes like?
I say she is more luscious than dates, fills your mouth with wisdom,
like mother's milk.

The women say you speak sweetly. Tell us where is this place?
I answer that it is greater than the black clouds shadowing the temples and
deeper than the rivers of dust they cross.

And the old women ask what do they believe in this place?
I tell them that we believe in the white horse and the wheel, and
though our souls are supple, like a young mare, the wheel turns for all.

Then the old men speak of war and ask who owns this place?
I reply that neither gold nor silver crosses our hands, nor do we bind one
another's necks for it. We rise every morning with ease, like a falcon, and
scatter freely like mist in the mountains.

Then the men argue and raise their swords—
and speak with all the shriveled tongues of the world,
and cry where are the coins and the continents? What of distrust and disease?
Who creates death there? Who sharpens the spear and where is the battle?

To which I reply with nothing… for there is nothing to be said.

Physics for the Perplexed

Not only is the Universe stranger than we think,
it is stranger than we can think.
　　　　—*Werner Heisenberg*

Once God was a clock
ringing infinitely.
The Watchmaker too.
He made music continuously.
Celestial, but unheard.

Eye of Newton,
and Schrodinger's cat.
One apple falls in Eden
and in Lincolnshire,
another, more enlightened,
falls further than that.

But what of gravity's pull?
Newton knew that God
had his prismatic notions,
found in light, not a trinity
of deified proportions.

Then, maybe God was a gambler
playing with dice,
Heisenberg's Uncertain
Principle allowing
a particle and wave
to both be right.

So, Gleick has his chaos,
Kaku his superstrings, and
Hawking all the blackholes
that a multiverse can bring.
Now we might say,
Whether there is a God or no,
We all must live in the unknowing of it all.

Voyage

I travel to a different country every day, to places
unentered by the fog and foam of the seaborne,
the rattle of mountain rails, or the wide sweep of the wind.

All the world, even its smallest creatures, visit
this impossible destination, never hearing
of the journeys each of us have taken.

I wonder at these curious tales, these impenetrable abodes,
where we seek a place of peace,
unreachable by any other compass or guide.

These reveries are as essential to my life
as the schools of learning I entered as a child.
They are a distant island younger than any memory I recollect.

With each return, I seek
those who traveled ahead of me.
And in the shadows of sleep, I see their stars.

Ferry

All too briefly we hold each other
    on this soft shore of recognition.

Yet I can't recall a moment when we weren't joined together,
    your hands interlaced with mine.

Rain makes the passage more intimate as
    clouds drape the mountains, a canopy over the sound.

Wind brings tender showers are an excuse for lovers, for us,
    to lean towards each other, a shelter from the sky.

Now, I see just over your shoulder
    the slow arc of a seagull streaming the currents.

We watch the ocean gently form mutable visions
    that whirl being out of nothingness.

Look at this love as varied as all the colors and countless
    creatures hidden beneath the sea's shale blue slice and swell.

You have so enfolded yourself into the place of things—
    this destination—your everywhere and all.

Which of us was foundling for the other? Whose heart leapt like dolphins
    twinned in joy, an enchantment of delight?

We are a little dreaming, both tidal and out of time,
    a storm set against a calm that pulls us ever back again.

Peace is a refugee...

stateless,
blanketing the barbed
wire and crawling underneath.
She knows the fears we guard and
sleeps in places desolate of love.
And drinks the embittered waters
we offer to the weak.
She knows how hungry,
how homeless our hearts,
how desperately we break the common
tongues we speak.

She is the setting for the wound,
the softening of the bruise.
And when our children
die upon each other's shores,
she gently pulls back the waves
and shows us what we once
were and our exiled fate.

If Peace Was a Postcard

She wouldn't have to do a thing
because every circumnavigated
stamp would wipe clean its posted face
and tug off and every destination would
run away and all the words would leave their
baggage behind and wriggle off the page
and run to her and say
Send me!
Send me!
Please, send me!

Beyond

Out beyond this needle,
this rain blotted landscape, evergreen,
beyond this shimmering city with
its hopes and its defeats,
beyond this state of emerald,
beyond all these nations with all
their little kings, beyond this blue planet
trying so damn hard to stay green,
beyond all those fleeting satellites that keep
our conversations to and froing underneath,
beyond all this, there is an immensity
of space where only stars can breathe.

With Thanks

My gratitude to my teachers, Jack Gilbert, Donna Masini, Colleen J. McElroy, Heather McHugh and Linda Bierds for sharing their illuminating insights.

And a deep thank you to John Sibley Williams for his astonishing critical acumen and wisdom when reading these pages. I owe you so very much.

I'd like to thank my husband, Greg Camenzind, and my daughter, Helena Camenzind, for providing time, love and support for me to write these poems. Thank you to my family, life companions, and friends beyond naming, both here and departed: thank you.

M. L. Lyons is a poet, writer and arts advocate. After being awarded a Klepser Fellowship at University of Washington, Lyons studied publishing at Simon Fraser University and interned at Copper Canyon Press. She has worked as a screenwriter and publicist in the entertainment industry, an editor for literary journals and a grants writer for literary arts organizations throughout the Pacific Northwest. She is co-editor of the award-winning poetry anthology, *Raising Lilly Ledbetter: Women Poets Occupy the Workplace*. Most recently she was awarded a scholarship for the Vortext Writing Retreat at Hedgebrook.